Witness

Shawn Pittard

A Publication of The Poetry Box®

Poems © 2024 Shawn Pittard
All rights reserved

Editing & Book Design by Shawn Aveningo Sanders
Cover Design by Robert R. Sanders
   using photograph by Shawn Pittard
Author Photo by Michael Kelly-DeWitt
Photo Editing by Robert R. Sanders

Witness was a finalist in The Poetry Box Chapbook Prize 2024

"Casting After Shadows" was first published in *Tule Review.*
"East Lawn" appeared the chapbook, *These Rivers* (Rattlesnake Press).

No part of this book may be republished without permission
from the author, except in the case of brief quotations
embodied in critical essays, epigraphs, reviews and articles,
or publisher/author's marketing collateral.

ISBN: 978-1-956285-77-2
Published in the United States of America
Wholesale Distribution by Ingram Group

Published by The Poetry Box, December 2024
Portland, Oregon, United States
website: ThePoetryBox.com

for Kathy

*and in memory of
Sharon & Glenn Pittard*

Contents

7 | Witness
8 | Winter's Hope
9 | Casting After Shadows
10 | Talking to the Darkness
12 | What the Waves Know
13 | The Peace Before Dreaming
14 | Another Fawn
15 | Marilee
16 | Stick with Me
17 | We Do This, We Do That
18 | Aging
19 | Anecdote
20 | Requiescat
21 | Since Your Death
22 | What's Become of My Parents
23 | I'm Thinking about Death
24 | East Lawn
28 | Good Night, Love

31 | Early Praise
33 | About the Author

Witness

My father knows something I don't.
Has seen something I haven't.
Been somewhere I have yet to go.

When he returned, his brown eyes
were blue-gray. He looks at me
from that distant place he visited.

Its gravity holds him
between the place where we talk
and the place where he was taken by the stroke.

He has important things to tell me
through the grip of his one good hand. Stories
I must not forget.

The boy left standing beside his mother
in the wheat field during harvest
after she collapsed under the weight of the sun.

The boy who spent an hour tying
and retying his necktie
before going into town to see a movie with his cousins.

The boy collecting payment
on his paper route—a handful of loose change
thrown into his face.

My father witnessed my birth.
I am witnessing his death.
We have something we must say.

Winter's Hope

Our fathers are dying.

My mother saw her father's spirit
rise up and out of his dead body.

I hoped for something similar
during the long hours of my father's death.

Death is everywhere today.
The birds are here to feast on it.

Trees bend under the weight of vultures—
black wings stretched

against the burnt-orange leaves of fall—
as spawned-out salmon drift downstream

and the still-living—
on their upstream mission to procreate—

dart urgently past my ankles.

Casting After Shadows

Spring blossoms fall
into their own reflections.

It's been a good year for the dogwood—
a bad year for the homeless.

I surprise a woman washing herself in the river.
We almost say hello.

My mother asked,
Why can't the dead at least come visit?

We were drinking coffee in the kitchen
before first light, before I stepped into the river,

before the sunrise lit the moving waters,
before the horned owl called our names.

Talking to the Darkness

1.

The longest night on earth. Winter solstice.
Tipped back on our axis as we orbit round the sun.

The cars with their booming basses are finally done cruising the street,
bumper-to-bumper, attracted by the sparkling Christmas lights.

The horses that drew the carriages have been brushed and put up for
  the night.
My mother tucked in with a kiss on the forehead.

2.

I am awake for the third time with nothing but the darkness to consult.
There's a prayer I can't remember that I don't say.

My mother says my father is watching over us.

He's come to me in a dream just once since his death.
Exhausted, he fell into my arms.

Another night he tapped on the dining room window.
Fiddled with the front-door lock.

I thought he'd come to take his sweetheart home. In the morning
she said she was visited "by a college boy with a beautiful smile."

3.

I miss that smile, too. I saw it when riding our motorcycles
into a lightning storm on the Continental Divide.

Hiking out on the hull of a screaming catamaran in the Gulf of
  California
just before the jib sail tore loose.

4.

After his stroke my father slept in the family room in a hospital bed.
My mother threw herself onto the floor next to it, wailing out her pain.

I picked her up and placed her in the single bed beside him.
Take me with you, my mother begged. *Take me with you.*

What the Waves Know

My mother was a lifeguard.
She taught her children how to swim.
She turned nineteen
the day before I was born.
She talks about young love
while we watch north coast waves
crash against the sea bluff.
Eighteen and pregnant,
playing in the surf with my dad.
Mom jokes
about me bodysurfing
while still in the womb.
I tell her that I miss my dad.
She says, I miss my husband.
Of the ocean, she says,
It just is. Just is.
The waves know
there is nothing to become.
We are all complete.
Nothing is missing.
One day I will return to the sea.
It would take me now
were I to wade into its cold embrace.
Take me now or take me later, it doesn't care.
How is it that I come to rest
in the presence of such relentless indifference?
If I ever grow old, I want to fall asleep
to the music of breaking waves.
I would like for that to be the last sound I hear.

The Peace Before Dreaming

Just when I thought I was easing into sleep
I heard my father's

one thousandth last breath
in the redwood timbers this house is built on.

His wife is sleeping safely here tonight—
my mother secure

despite confusion—moving toward the same inevitability
I am moving toward. I felt its

cold current wrap around my legs this morning
as I waded into water and fog.

Felt it when the stones rolled under my boots.
I am ready, I told the river gods.

And then what must have been one hundred geese descended,
first as sound, that honk and hink, then the beat of two hundred wings.

Another Fawn

This one dead in the thin grass
and late autumn leaves

on the bank beside the river named
for the Father, Son, and Holy Ghost

an incantation
I whisper three times

into its left ear
anticipating life

will spring back
into its slender body

and it will wobble up
onto its unsteady legs

the way it did
when it was first born.

*In the name of the Father,
the Son, and the Holy Ghost.*

The water is alive with salmon
and the rush of winter.

I touch the fawn's bony chest
the way I touched my father's

during the hours of his death.
Has he risen up

steadying himself somewhere
on the other side of the river.

Marilee

My mother gets a phone call from the past.
Her sister is dead. Something about a small plane,

fog, and the San Francisco Bay. Three boys
under eight years old—orphaned. "Marilee,

Marilee," she says, stirring in her sleep. "Marilee,
I promise I won't forget you."

Stick with Me

I came down the stairs to unplug the lights
on our Christmas tree. A feeling
something was undone awoke me.

The house was quiet.
My wife and mother asleep.
The mortgage almost paid.

More than once I've imagined this house in flames.
Burning to the ground.
Walking away with nothing but the shirt on my back.

After dinner tonight my mother said,
I'm not quite sure I know who I am.
I held her hand and said, Stick with me.

We Do This, We Do That

~inspired by Frank O'Hara

It took a while but we're comfortable now
with my helping her with her shower.

We're past the self-conscious joking.
We focus on the pleasures

of hot water, shampoo, and a bath sponge.
We take the time to scramble eggs

with parmesan, salt, and pepper.
Spend the rest of the morning cleaning up the kitchen.

Some days we go out to the wildlife area
with our binoculars and a couple of drive-through sodas

listening to rock-and-roll—
Mark Knopfler is a favorite but Elvis is the King.

During late afternoons, we tally up
the living and the dead:

a younger brother living and retired to the Philippines,
two of her big sister's three sons still alive;

among the dead her parents,
her husband of 62 years.

She says,
I'm your mother?

Yes, I'm your son.
But you're so old.

Aging

Seems like everyone is doing it.
Dying and dementia so common
they have become cliché.
Or so the burghers of poetry tell me.
Maybe I should write a poem about a man
who, on his 90th birthday, shuffles out
into the surf in the Great White waters
off Stinson Beach
straight toward a sun
setting like a Japanese war flag.
Wearing nothing but a lifejacket
and a fierce smile
he holds a Bowie knife in his right hand
a bloody steak to chum the waters in his left.
Or is that too melodramatic?

Anecdote

I went fishing on the Feather River with an old friend last Monday. In the parking lot at the Gridley Boat Launch we wriggled and wrestled ourselves into our waders. I was reminded of a guide named Pete we'd hired almost 15 years ago to float us down the Trinity. Pete could be described as robust. I asked my friend if he remembered that trip. He said yes, he remembered that trip. He also remembered my response to a question he asked me over a beer at the end of the day. He'd asked me what I thought about the quality of our guide. Would we hire Pete again? I said, I'd pay another $400 just to watch Pete struggle in and out of his waders at the boat launch. And there we were at a boat launch, struggling into our waders all those years later, putting on at least as good a show as Pete.

Requiescat

The river is drunk
on the tide's dark abundance.

An object in motion
stays in motion

My father's bright smile
is the reflection on black water.

unless acted upon
by an unbalanced force.

My mother's girl-blue eyes
are what's left of their future.

An object at rest
stays at rest.

We love and dream on the backs
of vast tectonic plates.

Standing on what feels like solid ground.

Since Your Death

The round song of the horned owl
is no longer an omen. I've stopped
waking to the least sound downstairs.
I listen for the night train now. To the wind
rustling crepe myrtle blossoms.
Watch for the new moon. Maybe
I am lonely. Open
in this moment to the mystery.
Vulnerable to its charms.
Sometimes we need a divine ear
that we can whisper into.

What's Become of My Parents?

Their bodies—
ash.

Still, I like to imagine them
carrying on where they left off
—but younger

before dementia—
making up for the time they lost.
Give them, at least, those years.

This is the hour in which one hopes.

Otherwise, I do not believe
the stories
about what happens next.

I do know
that I've heard two keys played
in the room where my mother
used to keep her piano.

I'm Thinking about Death

Not my death or your death
not even my mother's death
in my very arms but death itself

that voyeur always lurking
timebomb in the heart
seed of cancer in the sunburned nose

patient opportunist who I sometimes see
in the beaks of vultures
perched in the riverbank trees
or the angels etched into the frieze
at the cathedral.

Is it death who whispers *slow down*
when you should know there are deer
on the forest road this time of night?

Or says *go for it* when you look into the black water
from the jumping rock above the bridge.

East Lawn

1.

All night the great horned owl glides
the cemetery grounds, makes a hunting perch
of some grand monument.
By morning, he is gone.

It's the robins that are out, strutting
in their orange vests, yellow bills
pecking after earthworms
between blades of wet grass and headstones.

Then a flash of russet-colored tails,
Little claws clack on a redwood's furrowed bark.
A tease and chase across sunlight
burning off fog.
                      Everywhere,
the rut and strut of spring.

2.

I have been sitting a while
on a white marble bench.

Talking to no one.

Nearby, groundskeepers tell their jokes,
complain about the boss, talk on cell phones.

I feel pleasantly invisible.

Above me, the live oak's crooked branches
rise and fall
on the wind's steady breath.

3.

All winter—
below the iron gates of a mausoleum,
in a marble vase on the third granite step—
daffodil bulbs waited to bloom.

Some gardener cut those flowers back
the Monday after Easter—
the stems still moist.

4.

Someone placed a clutch of lilies
on a *beloved mother's* headstone.

Orange stamens, creamy petals—
white flames
flickering in the wind.

5.

Builder, scholar, poet-warrior,
beloved son and brother, daughter
of loving wife, mother & friend—
in God's care.

World War Veteran, native of
Armenia, Ireland, Watertown,
New York. Afgan
aged 30 years, born into heaven,
sleeping in Jesus' arms.

Born, married, died.

Here rests a Woodman of the World,
he will be dearly missed.

Servant of God—Friend of Man,
Wagoner, 145th Field Artillery,
rest in peace
until we meet again.

Papa, Dad, Father.
Born at Baden Germany,
Class of Harvard '97,
killed in action in Argonne,
ship's writer U.S. Coast Guard,
one of the Jones's Boys—
in the arms of angels may you fly.

Mama, Mommy, Mom.
Cherished Auntie.
Loyal Californian,
devoted to her family,

sacred to the memory,
our darling baby.

Sweetheart.

Infant son 1 day old
also buried here.

Of Such is the Kingdom of Heaven.

   6.

From our bed some nights, my wife and I hear
the round hoot of that great horned owl.

We lie closer now to that owl's night-song.
We lie awake—listening.

Good Night, Love

I say good night to the moon
because you do not lie beside me.
To the North Star. Orion's sparkling belt.
Good night to the streetlight. The lock
on the back door that I check twice.
Good night, love, I say to the place
in my heart where I carry you.
Good night, love, I will rest
with you one day.

Early Praise

The poems in Shawn Pittard's *Witness* offer us a world where every breath, every step could be the last, yet each also serves as revelation, a panorama, a shimmering strand in the web of connection and existence. With his broad cosmological perspective, he zeroes in with his poetic zoom lens to capture the challenges of aging, mortality, and loss—all the fragilities he encountered during years of daily caretaking for a beloved parent. These poems remind us how *We love and dream on the backs/ of vast tectonic plates.// Standing on what feels like solid ground.* (from "Requiescat")

—Susan Kelly-DeWitt, author of *Frangible Operas*

With these reflections Pittard invites us to appreciate the paradoxes raised by death—the mundane becoming the sacred; the losses, a gift; mortality AND joy. He shows a way to be open to the necessary contemplations at end-of-life—what does it mean to be on this life's ride and what is our place in the tapestry. A throughline of this collection emphasizes the mystery of connection—the ways we are and remain connected through intuition, touch, time, memory, dream, and inspirited energy—through this life and beyond death.

—Molly DenBoer Stuart, facilitator,
"Conversations About Death" programs

Shawn Pittard's book of poems, *Witness,* pays homage to his father and mother. It is a work of beautifully assembled words shaped around gratitude and respect. It is a book of sharing. Hard times/good times. It is a continuum. A collage of family moments hung on a wall at home. Deeply personal. A reflection. A celebration—Shawn opens the door and welcomes you to come inside.

—Danyen Powell, facilitator,
The Sacramento Poetry Center's Tuesday Night Poetry Workshop

About the Author

Shawn Pittard is the author of two slender volumes of poetry: *Standing in the River*, which was the winner of Tebot Bach's 2010 Clockwise Chapbook Competition, and *These Rivers* from Rattlesnake Press. He's been a coach for Poetry Out Loud and a California Poet in the Schools. Shawn taught recitation and writing in middle schools and high schools, including juvenile hall (yep, they're good kids), as well as with veterans and the men in Folsom Prison. By day, he labored in the field of environmental protection, planning, and public policy, focusing on energy.

About The Poetry Box®

The Poetry Box, a boutique publishing company in Portland, Oregon, provides a platform for both established and emerging poets to share their words with the world through beautiful printed books and chapbooks.

Feel free to visit the online bookstore (thePoetryBox.com), where you'll find more titles including:

Kansas, Reimagined by Anara Guard

The Squannacook at Dawn by Richard Jordan

Inside Out by Kirsten Morgan

Reading Wind by Carol Barrett

Now Is What Matters by Janet Steward

Journey of Trees by Susan Landgraf

Vitals & Other Signs of Life by David A. Goodrum

Rescue Dogs by Fred Zirm

When All Else Fails by Lana Hechtman Ayers

White Sail at Midnight by Ginny Lowe Connors

A Nest in the Heart by Vivienne Popperl

What She Was Wearing by Shawn Aveningo Sanders

Lamplight by Cathy Cain

Listening in the Dark by Suzy Harris

Building a Woman by Deborah Meltvedt

and many more . . .